The Shaman's Dream

Created By

Dakota Earth Cloud Walker

ISBN: 0692352104
ISBN-13: 978-0692352106

DEDICATION

To all the souls who have dared to
journey deep, trudge through the
lessons, and grow their soul.
You know who you are ....

TABLE OF CONTENTS

ACKNOWLEDGMENTS

To Amber, for being my rock while on my journey through life.

To all the members of the Shamanic Journeyers Club, thank you for your dedication and commitment to your own soul growth.

To the Spirits of the East,
thank you for your clarity and guidance.

To the Spirits of the South,
thank you for your nurturance and safe space to grow.

To the Spirits of the West,
thank you for your fires of transformation.

To the Spirits of the North,
thank you for your great guidance and counsel.

To the Spirit within me,
thank you for always being the beacon of light pointing home.

To Father Sky,
I give you my prayers.

To Mother Earth,
I give you my deepest respect.

And to all my Spirit Guides, Helping Animals, and to all my Ancestors, and Elders...

Aho Mitakuye Oyasin.

About Shamanic Journeyers Club

Shamanic Journeyers Club is a membership based community of like minded people who are dedicated to soul growth, shamanic studies, and using guided shamanic journeying as a tool for enriching their spiritual life.

To learn more about SJC please visit our website at:

www.shamanicjourneyersclub.com

"We breathe deeply into our experiences, the deep breath of "I Am" and in those moments of parting the veil our soul travels on the exhale weaving itself through time and space.

This is the place we come to in order to change the world, and to change ourselves.

Dropping the ego body we transcend into who we were born to become.

Go now .... Dream wide, journey far, and come home to your soul. Be renewed in this human experience once again. "

-Dakota Earth Cloud Walker-

Dreamtime of the Shaman

Dreamtime is the transpersonal reality beyond this world. It sits outside the realm of time. In our dreams we can visit other people, such as the deceased and other worlds. We can freely go backwards and forwards in time. We even visit places we have never imagined or seen in our waking life.

Dreamtime is the origin of everything.

In our modern world, we can compare the dream world to the internet – Hop on the internet and you can go anywhere in the world! You can research any answer, ask any question, and meet people you may never have been able to meet had it not been for the internet. You can learn new languages... you can do just about anything. And our dreams are the same .... Dreams can expand our humanity by expanding our world view.

There are several ways in which we can dream ...

1. Sleeping dreams
2. Shamanic Journeying
3. Re-Entry Dreams
4. Lucid Dreaming
5. Shamanic or Conscious Soul Breathing
6. Meditation

Sleeping Dreams

We spend 1/3 of our life asleep. What if we utilized that time to do something soulful and meaningful? Our dreams are a way for our subconscious mind to work through some of our life dilemmas and sync our soul back to our Divinity. Remembering your sleeping dreams can often help you resolve conflicts in your life, and also give you insight into what you may be dealing with or needing to address. By tracking your dreams, you can look for patterns or symbolism that give further meaning for you.

Shamanic Journeying

Shamanic Journeying takes a certain beat which entrains the brain to go into a theta state – in theta, shamans can travel the worlds, through time and space, and into non-ordinary reality. These can also be interpreted as disciplined voluntary dreams without ordinary reality guidance meaning. They are not guided imagery. During a Shamanic Journey, you may encounter your power and helping animals, helping spirits, ancestors, divine beings, and more. It is more than "imagining" something taking place; in a Shamanic Journey, your senses should be engaged to the point you can feel, hear, smell, see, and taste in these other dimensions.

Re-Entry Dreams

Dreams from our past or even a photo can become a portal for re-entry into the dream or the landscape and recover parts of your lost soul.

You need 3 things to do a Re-Entry.

1. **Doorway**—A dream which evokes great emotion and/or has vivid imagery. The best dreams for Re-Entry are ones which bring up a lot of energy for you. You will use this as the doorway to a certain place.

2. **Intention**—Whenever we travel back into a dream, we do so with a clear intention. Your intentions can be "What do I need to know?" and "What will I do once I'm in the dream?" You may want to solicit the help of a trusted ally or Spirit Guide to accompany you on the journey.

3. **Vehicle**—You cannot travel anywhere without a vehicle. Using either the drum beat used in Shamanic Journeying, music with binaural beats to help you reach Theta or Breathwork as a vehicle will help you to find the portal to re-enter your dream.

Lucid Dreaming

Lucid dreaming is the act of being aware while you are inside a dream. It has been described as being able to exist in 2 universes at the same time. You can explore your own consciousness as well as global consciousness. Lucid Dreaming takes persistence and practice, and it can be very rewarding to not be confined by the laws which govern our 3rd dimensional reality.

Shamanic Breathwork

Using Shamanic Breathwork or some form of Breathwork can help induce a theta and/or altered state. In many languages, the word "breath" translates to "soul" and is the vehicle most often used in achieving the altered state. There are several forms of Breathwork available. Try different ones to see which one works best for you.

Guided Meditation

Using guided meditation with well thought out intentions can help you to enter into the dreamscape to receive guidance, messages, and to meet with your helping spirits.

Soul Recovery Through Dreams

Soul loss occurs whenever there has been trauma or illness, sudden changes, etc. which cause your soul to escape the pain of being in the body. People who are abused, or in car accidents, or experience a sudden and tragic loss in their life – these are the type of events where your soul would leave to protect you either from physical or mental or emotional pain.

Dreams – whether waking or sleeping, for soul recovery, is an extraordinary tool. In typical, indigenous tribes and even in many teachings today people would go to the Shaman to retrieve parts of their soul that had been lost. The Shaman would journey (soul retrieval) often to the middle world, retrieve the soul parts, and bring them back to the person and blow them back into the body.

As we awaken to our divinity, we step back into our power and awaken the inner shaman within us. Instead of giving away our power by asking someone to retrieve our soul for us, we do our own soul recovery using conscious dream work and journeying.

Dreams are the gateway to travel back in time, even to past lives, to recover parts of our soul, and we can perform a "soul capture" where we give back the soul parts we have taken from others.

Sometimes we have dreams which indicate where we have lost our soul, and other times we produce the dreams by going back to a dream as an entry point. If you have been someplace in a dream, you can always return to it.

Using this Journey Journal

Using your time in dream-space and in journeys can be deeply moving and provide you with enormous soul growth. Being disciplined in recording your dreams will be very rewarding in the long run. Here are some guidelines for getting the most out of your journeys:

1. **Be clear with your intentions**. Even in your sleeping dreams you can formulate a clear intention prior to going to bed. Your intention might be to remember your dreams clearly or to work on a certain issue in your life. When you have clear intentions, the Universe will help deliver what you need. Keep your intentions in the framework of working outside the space/time continuum. Our guides don't work in linear time so asking a question about "when" something is going to happen will not work in a non-ordinary reality. Great questions begin with How,

what, or why ...

2. **Record your journey** or dream right after you have come out of your dream/journey state and before speaking to anyone. This is when it is the freshest and details will start to diminish the more engaged you become in ordinary reality. If you have a hard time remembering the details, lie back down and relax, let some images reappear and try to thread some pieces together. If you need to, record some highlights that will jolt your memory later.

3. **Keep your tools handy**—have a pen, this journal, a small light nearby for recording as soon as you wake up or come out of your journey.

4. **Don't be the censor or the judge!** When recording, record just the facts and the experiences. Don't leave anything out, don't change something to make it better or worse. Don't analyze or judge it. The cleaner the reporting is, the more honest the messages will be.

5. **Refrain from asking others to interpret** your journeys for you. If you are in a workshop or doing a Shamanic Breathwork session, then there typically will be some feedback from the facilitator about your session; however, even in those times, you are truly the one who holds the key. Your helping spirits and the Divine spirits know you intimately and will communicate in a language that only you will understand. Anyone else will be filtering their interpretations through their own set of life filters which, more than likely, will have no resemblance to your own. If you still don't understand a message or meaning

then take it to your next journey or meditation and ask your Spirit Guides to clarify the meaning for you. Never give your power away to someone else by letting them tell you what your experience means or doesn't mean.

6. **Create sacred space.** When you meditate or journey, the work begins before your session ever does. Create the space in your life, be sure to be in uninterrupted space, create an altar of things that are special to you. Do the same for your bedroom where you sleep—clear the space, take out as many electronics as you can from your bedroom. This frees the energy from electromagnetic energy. If you are sleeping amidst clutter, then your sleeping life will feel cluttered as well.

7. **Ask for guidance.** Your spirit guides and helping spirits are here to help you and to guide you. Ask them for their support. Create a sacred relationship with them, get to know them, and learn how they communicate to you and with you.

You can learn more about dreaming, shamanic journeying, breathwork, soul recovery, and soul capturing through our online course: *Dreaming Our Soul Home.*

To register go to www.shamanicjourneyersclub.com

Nugget of Truth:

Use this space to write down what this dream or journey has taught you or the insight you gained from it.

More Dream Notes:

Example Entry

Title: You can title your dream or the name of the journey you took

Date:

Type: ☐ Lucid   ☐ Meditation   ☐ Sleeping   ☐ Re-Entry
☐ Shamanic Journey   ☐ Breathwork

Mood: ☐ Pleasant   ☐ Neutral ☐ Unpleasant

Emotions: ☐ Anger ☐ Fear ☐ Frustration ☐ Loneliness ☐ Grief

☐ Sadness   ☐ Surprise ☐ Jealousy ☐ Disgust ☐ Joy ☐ Happiness

☐ Curiosity ☐ Love ☐ Sexual ☐ _____ ☐ _____ ☐ _____

Key Words/Elements: Use key words like you would use "tags" so you can

start looking for patterns in your dreams.

Symbols: Were there any symbols, shapes, symbolic items, etc. that

showed up in your dream/journey?

People/Spirits: Who was in the dream/journey with you? What spirit

guides or helping spirits came through? Ancestors?

Place: Either a real place, upper, lower, or middle world or maybe a place in time.

Your Role: Were you the main character or an observer? Young or older?

Storyline: Tell the story of your dream here, use the note area on the

facing page if you need more room.

☐ Use this journey for future re-entry?

May Your Journey Begin ....

This journal belongs to:

_____

Dates of Entries:

____/____/____ to ____/____/____

Nugget of Truth:

More Dream Notes:

Title:

Date:

Type: ☐ Lucid ☐ Meditation ☐ Sleeping ☐ Re-Entry
☐ Shamanic Journey ☐ Breathwork

Mood: ☐ Pleasant ☐ Neutral ☐ Unpleasant

Emotions: ☐ Anger ☐ Fear ☐ Frustration ☐ Loneliness ☐ Grief

☐ Sadness ☐ Surprise ☐ Jealousy ☐ Disgust ☐ Joy ☐ Happiness

☐ Curiosity ☐ Love ☐ Sexual ☐ _____ ☐ _____ ☐ _____

Key Words/Elements:

Symbols:

People/Spirits:

Place:

Your Role:

Storyline:

☐ Use this journey for future re-entry?

Nugget of Truth:

More Dream Notes:

Title:

Date:

Type: ☐ Lucid   ☐ Meditation   ☐ Sleeping   ☐ Re-Entry
☐ Shamanic Journey   ☐ Breathwork

Mood: ☐ Pleasant   ☐ Neutral   ☐ Unpleasant

Emotions: ☐ Anger   ☐ Fear ☐ Frustration ☐ Loneliness ☐ Grief

☐ Sadness   ☐ Surprise ☐ Jealousy ☐ Disgust ☐ Joy ☐ Happiness

☐ Curiosity ☐ Love ☐ Sexual ☐ _____ ☐ _____ ☐ _____

Key Words/Elements:

Symbols:

People/Spirits:

Place:

Your Role:

Storyline:

☐ Use this journey for future re-entry?

Nugget of Truth:

More Dream Notes:

Title:

Date:

Type: ☐ Lucid   ☐ Meditation   ☐ Sleeping   ☐ Re-Entry
☐ Shamanic Journey   ☐ Breathwork

Mood: ☐ Pleasant   ☐ Neutral   ☐ Unpleasant

Emotions: ☐ Anger ☐ Fear ☐ Frustration ☐ Loneliness ☐ Grief

☐ Sadness   ☐ Surprise ☐ Jealousy ☐ Disgust ☐ Joy ☐ Happiness

☐ Curiosity ☐ Love ☐ Sexual ☐ _____   ☐ _____   ☐ _____

Key Words/Elements:

Symbols:

People/Spirits:

Place:

Your Role:

Storyline:

☐ Use this journey for future re-entry?

Nugget of Truth:

More Dream Notes:

Title:

Date:

Type: ☐ Lucid ☐ Meditation ☐ Sleeping ☐ Re-Entry
☐ Shamanic Journey ☐ Breathwork

Mood: ☐ Pleasant ☐ Neutral ☐ Unpleasant

Emotions: ☐ Anger ☐ Fear ☐ Frustration ☐ Loneliness ☐ Grief

☐ Sadness ☐ Surprise ☐ Jealousy ☐ Disgust ☐ Joy ☐ Happiness

☐ Curiosity ☐ Love ☐ Sexual ☐ _____ ☐ _____ ☐ _____

Key Words/Elements:

Symbols:

People/Spirits:

Place:

Your Role:

Storyline:

☐ Use this journey for future re-entry?

Nugget of Truth:

More Dream Notes:

Title:

Date:

Type: ☐ Lucid   ☐ Meditation   ☐ Sleeping   ☐ Re-Entry
☐ Shamanic Journey   ☐ Breathwork

Mood: ☐ Pleasant ☐ Neutral ☐ Unpleasant

Emotions: ☐ Anger ☐ Fear ☐ Frustration ☐ Loneliness ☐ Grief

☐ Sadness ☐ Surprise ☐ Jealousy ☐ Disgust ☐ Joy ☐ Happiness

☐ Curiosity ☐ Love ☐ Sexual ☐ _____ ☐ _____ ☐ _____

Key Words/Elements:

Symbols:

People/Spirits:

Place:

Your Role:

Storyline:

☐ Use this journey for future re-entry?

Nugget of Truth:

More Dream Notes:

Title:

Date:

Type: ☐ Lucid   ☐ Meditation   ☐ Sleeping   ☐ Re-Entry
☐ Shamanic Journey   ☐ Breathwork

Mood: ☐ Pleasant   ☐ Neutral ☐ Unpleasant

Emotions: ☐ Anger   ☐ Fear ☐ Frustration ☐ Loneliness ☐ Grief

☐ Sadness   ☐ Surprise ☐ Jealousy ☐ Disgust ☐ Joy ☐ Happiness

☐ Curiosity ☐ Love ☐ Sexual ☐ _____ ☐ _____ ☐ _____

Key Words/Elements:

Symbols:

People/Spirits:

Place:

Your Role:

Storyline:

☐ Use this journey for future re-entry?

Nugget of Truth:

More Dream Notes:

Title:

Date:

Type: ☐ Lucid ☐ Meditation ☐ Sleeping ☐ Re-Entry
☐ Shamanic Journey ☐ Breathwork

Mood: ☐ Pleasant ☐ Neutral ☐ Unpleasant

Emotions: ☐ Anger ☐ Fear ☐ Frustration ☐ Loneliness ☐ Grief

☐ Sadness ☐ Surprise ☐ Jealousy ☐ Disgust ☐ Joy ☐ Happiness

☐ Curiosity ☐ Love ☐ Sexual ☐ _____ ☐ _____ ☐ _____

Key Words/Elements:

Symbols:

People/Spirits:

Place:

Your Role:

Storyline:

☐ Use this journey for future re-entry?

Nugget of Truth:

More Dream Notes:

Title:

Date:

Type: ☐ Lucid ☐ Meditation ☐ Sleeping ☐ Re-Entry
☐ Shamanic Journey ☐ Breathwork

Mood: ☐ Pleasant ☐ Neutral ☐ Unpleasant

Emotions: ☐ Anger ☐ Fear ☐ Frustration ☐ Loneliness ☐ Grief

☐ Sadness ☐ Surprise ☐ Jealousy ☐ Disgust ☐ Joy ☐ Happiness

☐ Curiosity ☐ Love ☐ Sexual ☐ _____ ☐ _____ ☐ _____

Key Words/Elements:

Symbols:

People/Spirits:

Place:

Your Role:

Storyline:

☐ Use this journey for future re-entry?

Nugget of Truth:

More Dream Notes:

Title:

Date:

Type: ☐ Lucid ☐ Meditation ☐ Sleeping ☐ Re-Entry
☐ Shamanic Journey ☐ Breathwork

Mood: ☐ Pleasant ☐ Neutral ☐ Unpleasant

Emotions: ☐ Anger ☐ Fear ☐ Frustration ☐ Loneliness ☐ Grief

☐ Sadness ☐ Surprise ☐ Jealousy ☐ Disgust ☐ Joy ☐ Happiness

☐ Curiosity ☐ Love ☐ Sexual ☐ _____ ☐ _____ ☐ _____

Key Words/Elements:

Symbols:

People/Spirits:

Place:

Your Role:

Storyline:

☐ Use this journey for future re-entry?

Nugget of Truth:

More Dream Notes:

Title:

Date:

Type: ☐ Lucid   ☐ Meditation   ☐ Sleeping   ☐ Re-Entry
☐ Shamanic Journey   ☐ Breathwork

Mood: ☐ Pleasant   ☐ Neutral   ☐ Unpleasant

Emotions: ☐ Anger   ☐ Fear   ☐ Frustration   ☐ Loneliness   ☐ Grief

☐ Sadness   ☐ Surprise ☐ Jealousy ☐ Disgust ☐ Joy ☐ Happiness

☐ Curiosity ☐ Love ☐ Sexual ☐ _____   ☐ _____   ☐ _____

Key Words/Elements:

Symbols:

People/Spirits:

Place:

Your Role:

Storyline:

☐ Use this journey for future re-entry?

Nugget of Truth:

More Dream Notes:

Title:

Date:

Type: ☐ Lucid ☐ Meditation ☐ Sleeping ☐ Re-Entry
☐ Shamanic Journey ☐ Breathwork

Mood: ☐ Pleasant ☐ Neutral ☐ Unpleasant

Emotions: ☐ Anger ☐ Fear ☐ Frustration ☐ Loneliness ☐ Grief

☐ Sadness ☐ Surprise ☐ Jealousy ☐ Disgust ☐ Joy ☐ Happiness

☐ Curiosity ☐ Love ☐ Sexual ☐ _____ ☐ _____ ☐ _____

Key Words/Elements:

Symbols:

People/Spirits:

Place:

Your Role:

Storyline:

☐ Use this journey for future re-entry?

Nugget of Truth:

More Dream Notes:

Title:

Date:

Type: ☐ Lucid ☐ Meditation ☐ Sleeping ☐ Re-Entry
☐ Shamanic Journey ☐ Breathwork

Mood: ☐ Pleasant ☐ Neutral ☐ Unpleasant

Emotions: ☐ Anger ☐ Fear ☐ Frustration ☐ Loneliness ☐ Grief

☐ Sadness ☐ Surprise ☐ Jealousy ☐ Disgust ☐ Joy ☐ Happiness

☐ Curiosity ☐ Love ☐ Sexual ☐ _____ ☐ _____ ☐ _____

Key Words/Elements:

Symbols:

People/Spirits:

Place:

Your Role:

Storyline:

☐ Use this journey for future re-entry?

Nugget of Truth:

More Dream Notes:

Title:

Date:

Type: ☐ Lucid   ☐ Meditation   ☐ Sleeping   ☐ Re-Entry
☐ Shamanic Journey   ☐ Breathwork

Mood: ☐ Pleasant   ☐ Neutral   ☐ Unpleasant

Emotions: ☐ Anger ☐ Fear ☐ Frustration ☐ Loneliness ☐ Grief

☐ Sadness   ☐ Surprise ☐ Jealousy ☐ Disgust ☐ Joy ☐ Happiness

☐ Curiosity ☐ Love ☐ Sexual ☐ _____ ☐ _____ ☐ _____

Key Words/Elements:

Symbols:

People/Spirits:

Place:

Your Role:

Storyline:

☐ Use this journey for future re-entry?

Nugget of Truth:

More Dream Notes:

Title:

Date:

Type: ☐ Lucid ☐ Meditation ☐ Sleeping ☐ Re-Entry
☐ Shamanic Journey ☐ Breathwork

Mood: ☐ Pleasant ☐ Neutral ☐ Unpleasant

Emotions: ☐ Anger ☐ Fear ☐ Frustration ☐ Loneliness ☐ Grief

☐ Sadness ☐ Surprise ☐ Jealousy ☐ Disgust ☐ Joy ☐ Happiness

☐ Curiosity ☐ Love ☐ Sexual ☐ _____ ☐ _____ ☐ _____

Key Words/Elements:

Symbols:

People/Spirits:

Place:

Your Role:

Storyline:

☐ Use this journey for future re-entry?

Nugget of Truth:

More Dream Notes:

Title:

Date:

Type: ☐ Lucid ☐ Meditation ☐ Sleeping ☐ Re-Entry
☐ Shamanic Journey ☐ Breathwork

Mood: ☐ Pleasant ☐ Neutral ☐ Unpleasant

Emotions: ☐ Anger ☐ Fear ☐ Frustration ☐ Loneliness ☐ Grief

☐ Sadness ☐ Surprise ☐ Jealousy ☐ Disgust ☐ Joy ☐ Happiness

☐ Curiosity ☐ Love ☐ Sexual ☐ _____ ☐ _____ ☐ _____

Key Words/Elements:

Symbols:

People/Spirits:

Place:

Your Role:

Storyline:

☐ Use this journey for future re-entry?

Nugget of Truth:

More Dream Notes:

Title:

Date:

Type: ☐ Lucid   ☐ Meditation   ☐ Sleeping   ☐ Re-Entry
☐ Shamanic Journey   ☐ Breathwork

Mood: ☐ Pleasant   ☐ Neutral ☐ Unpleasant

Emotions: ☐ Anger   ☐ Fear ☐ Frustration ☐ Loneliness ☐ Grief

☐ Sadness   ☐ Surprise ☐ Jealousy ☐ Disgust ☐ Joy ☐ Happiness

☐ Curiosity ☐ Love   ☐ Sexual ☐ _____   ☐ _____   ☐ _____

Key Words/Elements:

Symbols:

People/Spirits:

Place:

Your Role:

Storyline:

☐ Use this journey for future re-entry?

Nugget of Truth:

More Dream Notes:

Title:

Date:

Type: ☐ Lucid ☐ Meditation ☐ Sleeping ☐ Re-Entry
☐ Shamanic Journey ☐ Breathwork

Mood: ☐ Pleasant ☐ Neutral ☐ Unpleasant

Emotions: ☐ Anger ☐ Fear ☐ Frustration ☐ Loneliness ☐ Grief

☐ Sadness ☐ Surprise ☐ Jealousy ☐ Disgust ☐ Joy ☐ Happiness

☐ Curiosity ☐ Love ☐ Sexual ☐ _____ ☐ _____ ☐ _____

Key Words/Elements:

Symbols:

People/Spirits:

Place:

Your Role:

Storyline:

☐ Use this journey for future re-entry?

Nugget of Truth:

More Dream Notes:

Title:

Date:

Type: ☐ Lucid ☐ Meditation ☐ Sleeping ☐ Re-Entry
☐ Shamanic Journey ☐ Breathwork

Mood: ☐ Pleasant ☐ Neutral ☐ Unpleasant

Emotions: ☐ Anger ☐ Fear ☐ Frustration ☐ Loneliness ☐ Grief

☐ Sadness ☐ Surprise ☐ Jealousy ☐ Disgust ☐ Joy ☐ Happiness

☐ Curiosity ☐ Love ☐ Sexual ☐ _____ ☐ _____ ☐ _____

Key Words/Elements:

Symbols:

People/Spirits:

Place:

Your Role:

Storyline:

☐ Use this journey for future re-entry?

Nugget of Truth:

More Dream Notes:

Title:

Date:

Type: ☐ Lucid ☐ Meditation ☐ Sleeping ☐ Re-Entry
☐ Shamanic Journey ☐ Breathwork

Mood: ☐ Pleasant ☐ Neutral ☐ Unpleasant

Emotions: ☐ Anger ☐ Fear ☐ Frustration ☐ Loneliness ☐ Grief

☐ Sadness ☐ Surprise ☐ Jealousy ☐ Disgust ☐ Joy ☐ Happiness

☐ Curiosity ☐ Love ☐ Sexual ☐ _____ ☐ _____ ☐ _____

Key Words/Elements:

Symbols:

People/Spirits:

Place:

Your Role:

Storyline:

☐ Use this journey for future re-entry?

Nugget of Truth:

More Dream Notes:

Title:

Date:

Type: ☐ Lucid ☐ Meditation ☐ Sleeping ☐ Re-Entry
☐ Shamanic Journey ☐ Breathwork

Mood: ☐ Pleasant ☐ Neutral ☐ Unpleasant

Emotions: ☐ Anger ☐ Fear ☐ Frustration ☐ Loneliness ☐ Grief

☐ Sadness ☐ Surprise ☐ Jealousy ☐ Disgust ☐ Joy ☐ Happiness

☐ Curiosity ☐ Love ☐ Sexual ☐ _____ ☐ _____ ☐ _____

Key Words/Elements:

Symbols:

People/Spirits:

Place:

Your Role:

Storyline:

☐ Use this journey for future re-entry?

Nugget of Truth:

More Dream Notes:

Title:

Date:

Type: ☐ Lucid   ☐ Meditation   ☐ Sleeping   ☐ Re-Entry
☐ Shamanic Journey   ☐ Breathwork

Mood: ☐ Pleasant ☐ Neutral ☐ Unpleasant

Emotions: ☐ Anger ☐ Fear ☐ Frustration ☐ Loneliness ☐ Grief

☐ Sadness ☐ Surprise ☐ Jealousy ☐ Disgust ☐ Joy ☐ Happiness

☐ Curiosity ☐ Love ☐ Sexual ☐ _____ ☐ _____ ☐ _____

Key Words/Elements:

Symbols:

People/Spirits:

Place:

Your Role:

Storyline:

☐ Use this journey for future re-entry?

Nugget of Truth:

More Dream Notes:

Title:

Date:

Type: ☐ Lucid   ☐ Meditation   ☐ Sleeping   ☐ Re-Entry
☐ Shamanic Journey   ☐ Breathwork

Mood: ☐ Pleasant ☐ Neutral ☐ Unpleasant

Emotions: ☐ Anger ☐ Fear ☐ Frustration ☐ Loneliness ☐ Grief

☐ Sadness ☐ Surprise ☐ Jealousy ☐ Disgust ☐ Joy ☐ Happiness

☐ Curiosity ☐ Love ☐ Sexual ☐ _____ ☐ _____ ☐ _____

Key Words/Elements:

Symbols:

People/Spirits:

Place:

Your Role:

Storyline:

☐ Use this journey for future re-entry?

Nugget of Truth:

More Dream Notes:

Title:

Date:

Type: ☐ Lucid ☐ Meditation ☐ Sleeping ☐ Re-Entry
☐ Shamanic Journey ☐ Breathwork

Mood: ☐ Pleasant ☐ Neutral ☐ Unpleasant

Emotions: ☐ Anger ☐ Fear ☐ Frustration ☐ Loneliness ☐ Grief

☐ Sadness ☐ Surprise ☐ Jealousy ☐ Disgust ☐ Joy ☐ Happiness

☐ Curiosity ☐ Love ☐ Sexual ☐ _____ ☐ _____ ☐ _____

Key Words/Elements:

Symbols:

People/Spirits:

Place:

Your Role:

Storyline:

☐ Use this journey for future re-entry?

Nugget of Truth:

More Dream Notes:

Title:

Date:

Type: ☐ Lucid   ☐ Meditation   ☐ Sleeping   ☐ Re-Entry
☐ Shamanic Journey   ☐ Breathwork

Mood: ☐ Pleasant ☐ Neutral ☐ Unpleasant

Emotions: ☐ Anger ☐ Fear ☐ Frustration ☐ Loneliness ☐ Grief

☐ Sadness ☐ Surprise ☐ Jealousy ☐ Disgust ☐ Joy ☐ Happiness

☐ Curiosity ☐ Love ☐ Sexual ☐ _____ ☐ _____ ☐ _____

Key Words/Elements:

Symbols:

People/Spirits:

Place:

Your Role:

Storyline:

☐ Use this journey for future re-entry?

Nugget of Truth:

More Dream Notes:

Title:

Date:

Type: ☐ Lucid   ☐ Meditation   ☐ Sleeping   ☐ Re-Entry
       ☐ Shamanic Journey   ☐ Breathwork

Mood: ☐ Pleasant   ☐ Neutral   ☐ Unpleasant

Emotions: ☐ Anger   ☐ Fear   ☐ Frustration   ☐ Loneliness   ☐ Grief

☐ Sadness   ☐ Surprise ☐ Jealousy ☐ Disgust ☐ Joy ☐ Happiness

☐ Curiosity ☐ Love   ☐ Sexual ☐ _____   ☐ _____   ☐ _____

Key Words/Elements:

Symbols:

People/Spirits:

Place:

Your Role:

Storyline:

☐ Use this journey for future re-entry?

Nugget of Truth:

More Dream Notes:

Title:

Date:

Type: ☐ Lucid   ☐ Meditation ☐ Sleeping   ☐ Re-Entry
☐ Shamanic Journey   ☐ Breathwork

Mood: ☐ Pleasant ☐ Neutral ☐ Unpleasant

Emotions: ☐ Anger ☐ Fear ☐ Frustration ☐ Loneliness ☐ Grief

☐ Sadness   ☐ Surprise ☐ Jealousy ☐ Disgust ☐ Joy ☐ Happiness

☐ Curiosity ☐ Love ☐ Sexual ☐ _____ ☐ _____ ☐ _____

Key Words/Elements:

Symbols:

People/Spirits:

Place:

Your Role:

Storyline:

☐ Use this journey for future re-entry?

Nugget of Truth:

More Dream Notes:

Title:

Date:

Type: □ Lucid □ Meditation □ Sleeping □ Re-Entry
□ Shamanic Journey □ Breathwork

Mood: □ Pleasant □ Neutral □ Unpleasant

Emotions: □ Anger □ Fear □ Frustration □ Loneliness □ Grief

□ Sadness □ Surprise □ Jealousy □ Disgust □ Joy □ Happiness

□ Curiosity □ Love □ Sexual □ _____ □ _____ □ _____

Key Words/Elements:

Symbols:

People/Spirits:

Place:

Your Role:

Storyline:

□ Use this journey for future re-entry?

Nugget of Truth:

More Dream Notes:

Title:

Date:

Type: ☐ Lucid ☐ Meditation ☐ Sleeping ☐ Re-Entry
☐ Shamanic Journey ☐ Breathwork

Mood: ☐ Pleasant ☐ Neutral ☐ Unpleasant

Emotions: ☐ Anger ☐ Fear ☐ Frustration ☐ Loneliness ☐ Grief

☐ Sadness ☐ Surprise ☐ Jealousy ☐ Disgust ☐ Joy ☐ Happiness

☐ Curiosity ☐ Love ☐ Sexual ☐ _____ ☐ _____ ☐ _____

Key Words/Elements:

Symbols:

People/Spirits:

Place:

Your Role:

Storyline:

☐ Use this journey for future re-entry?

Nugget of Truth:

More Dream Notes:

Title:

Date:

Type: ☐ Lucid ☐ Meditation ☐ Sleeping ☐ Re-Entry
☐ Shamanic Journey ☐ Breathwork

Mood: ☐ Pleasant ☐ Neutral ☐ Unpleasant

Emotions: ☐ Anger ☐ Fear ☐ Frustration ☐ Loneliness ☐ Grief

☐ Sadness ☐ Surprise ☐ Jealousy ☐ Disgust ☐ Joy ☐ Happiness

☐ Curiosity ☐ Love ☐ Sexual ☐ _____ ☐ _____ ☐ _____

Key Words/Elements:

Symbols:

People/Spirits:

Place:

Your Role:

Storyline:

☐ Use this journey for future re-entry?

Nugget of Truth:

More Dream Notes:

Title:

Date:

Type: ☐ Lucid   ☐ Meditation   ☐ Sleeping   ☐ Re-Entry
       ☐ Shamanic Journey   ☐ Breathwork

Mood: ☐ Pleasant   ☐ Neutral ☐ Unpleasant

Emotions: ☐ Anger ☐ Fear ☐ Frustration ☐ Loneliness ☐ Grief

☐ Sadness   ☐ Surprise ☐ Jealousy ☐ Disgust ☐ Joy ☐ Happiness

☐ Curiosity ☐ Love ☐ Sexual ☐ _____ ☐ _____ ☐ _____

Key Words/Elements:

Symbols:

People/Spirits:

Place:

Your Role:

Storyline:

☐ Use this journey for future re-entry?

81

Nugget of Truth:

More Dream Notes:

Title:

Date:

Type: ☐ Lucid ☐ Meditation ☐ Sleeping ☐ Re-Entry
☐ Shamanic Journey ☐ Breathwork

Mood: ☐ Pleasant ☐ Neutral ☐ Unpleasant

Emotions: ☐ Anger ☐ Fear ☐ Frustration ☐ Loneliness ☐ Grief

☐ Sadness ☐ Surprise ☐ Jealousy ☐ Disgust ☐ Joy ☐ Happiness

☐ Curiosity ☐ Love ☐ Sexual ☐ _____ ☐ _____ ☐ _____

Key Words/Elements:

Symbols:

People/Spirits:

Place:

Your Role:

Storyline:

☐ Use this journey for future re-entry?

Nugget of Truth:

More Dream Notes:

Title:

Date:

Type: ☐ Lucid   ☐ Meditation ☐ Sleeping ☐ Re-Entry
☐ Shamanic Journey   ☐ Breathwork

Mood: ☐ Pleasant ☐ Neutral ☐ Unpleasant

Emotions: ☐ Anger ☐ Fear ☐ Frustration ☐ Loneliness ☐ Grief

☐ Sadness   ☐ Surprise ☐ Jealousy ☐ Disgust ☐ Joy ☐ Happiness

☐ Curiosity ☐ Love ☐ Sexual ☐ _____   ☐ _____   ☐ _____

Key Words/Elements:

Symbols:

People/Spirits:

Place:

Your Role:

Storyline:

☐ Use this journey for future re-entry?

Nugget of Truth:

More Dream Notes:

Title:

Date:

Type: ☐ Lucid ☐ Meditation ☐ Sleeping ☐ Re-Entry
☐ Shamanic Journey ☐ Breathwork

Mood: ☐ Pleasant ☐ Neutral ☐ Unpleasant

Emotions: ☐ Anger ☐ Fear ☐ Frustration ☐ Loneliness ☐ Grief

☐ Sadness ☐ Surprise ☐ Jealousy ☐ Disgust ☐ Joy ☐ Happiness

☐ Curiosity ☐ Love ☐ Sexual ☐ _____ ☐ _____ ☐ _____

Key Words/Elements:

Symbols:

People/Spirits:

Place:

Your Role:

Storyline:

☐ Use this journey for future re-entry?

Nugget of Truth:

More Dream Notes:

Title:

Date:

Type: ☐ Lucid ☐ Meditation ☐ Sleeping ☐ Re-Entry
☐ Shamanic Journey ☐ Breathwork

Mood: ☐ Pleasant ☐ Neutral ☐ Unpleasant

Emotions: ☐ Anger ☐ Fear ☐ Frustration ☐ Loneliness ☐ Grief

☐ Sadness ☐ Surprise ☐ Jealousy ☐ Disgust ☐ Joy ☐ Happiness

☐ Curiosity ☐ Love ☐ Sexual ☐ _____ ☐ _____ ☐ _____

Key Words/Elements:

Symbols:

People/Spirits:

Place:

Your Role:

Storyline:

☐ Use this journey for future re-entry?

Nugget of Truth:

More Dream Notes:

Title:

Date:

Type: ☐ Lucid ☐ Meditation ☐ Sleeping ☐ Re-Entry
☐ Shamanic Journey ☐ Breathwork

Mood: ☐ Pleasant ☐ Neutral ☐ Unpleasant

Emotions: ☐ Anger ☐ Fear ☐ Frustration ☐ Loneliness ☐ Grief

☐ Sadness ☐ Surprise ☐ Jealousy ☐ Disgust ☐ Joy ☐ Happiness

☐ Curiosity ☐ Love ☐ Sexual ☐ _____ ☐ _____ ☐ _____

Key Words/Elements:

Symbols:

People/Spirits:

Place:

Your Role:

Storyline:

☐ Use this journey for future re-entry?

Nugget of Truth:

More Dream Notes:

Title:

Date:

Type: ☐ Lucid ☐ Meditation ☐ Sleeping ☐ Re-Entry
☐ Shamanic Journey ☐ Breathwork

Mood: ☐ Pleasant ☐ Neutral ☐ Unpleasant

Emotions: ☐ Anger ☐ Fear ☐ Frustration ☐ Loneliness ☐ Grief

☐ Sadness ☐ Surprise ☐ Jealousy ☐ Disgust ☐ Joy ☐ Happiness

☐ Curiosity ☐ Love ☐ Sexual ☐ _____ ☐ _____ ☐ _____

Key Words/Elements:

Symbols:

People/Spirits:

Place:

Your Role:

Storyline:

☐ Use this journey for future re-entry?

Nugget of Truth:

More Dream Notes:

Title:

Date:

Type: ☐ Lucid ☐ Meditation ☐ Sleeping ☐ Re-Entry
☐ Shamanic Journey ☐ Breathwork

Mood: ☐ Pleasant ☐ Neutral ☐ Unpleasant

Emotions: ☐ Anger ☐ Fear ☐ Frustration ☐ Loneliness ☐ Grief

☐ Sadness ☐ Surprise ☐ Jealousy ☐ Disgust ☐ Joy ☐ Happiness

☐ Curiosity ☐ Love ☐ Sexual ☐ _____ ☐ _____ ☐ _____

Key Words/Elements:

Symbols:

People/Spirits:

Place:

Your Role:

Storyline:

☐ Use this journey for future re-entry?

Nugget of Truth:

More Dream Notes:

Title:

Date:

Type: ☐ Lucid   ☐ Meditation ☐ Sleeping ☐ Re-Entry
☐ Shamanic Journey   ☐ Breathwork

Mood: ☐ Pleasant ☐ Neutral ☐ Unpleasant

Emotions: ☐ Anger ☐ Fear ☐ Frustration ☐ Loneliness ☐ Grief

☐ Sadness ☐ Surprise ☐ Jealousy ☐ Disgust ☐ Joy ☐ Happiness

☐ Curiosity ☐ Love ☐ Sexual ☐ _____ ☐ _____ ☐ _____

Key Words/Elements:

Symbols:

People/Spirits:

Place:

Your Role:

Storyline:

☐ Use this journey for future re-entry?

Nugget of Truth:

More Dream Notes:

Title:

Date:

Type: ☐ Lucid ☐ Meditation ☐ Sleeping ☐ Re-Entry
☐ Shamanic Journey ☐ Breathwork

Mood: ☐ Pleasant ☐ Neutral ☐ Unpleasant

Emotions: ☐ Anger ☐ Fear ☐ Frustration ☐ Loneliness ☐ Grief

☐ Sadness ☐ Surprise ☐ Jealousy ☐ Disgust ☐ Joy ☐ Happiness

☐ Curiosity ☐ Love ☐ Sexual ☐ _____ ☐ _____ ☐ _____

Key Words/Elements:

Symbols:

People/Spirits:

Place:

Your Role:

Storyline:

☐ Use this journey for future re-entry?

Nugget of Truth:

More Dream Notes:

Title:

Date:

Type: ☐ Lucid   ☐ Meditation ☐ Sleeping ☐ Re-Entry
☐ Shamanic Journey   ☐ Breathwork

Mood: ☐ Pleasant ☐ Neutral ☐ Unpleasant

Emotions: ☐ Anger ☐ Fear ☐ Frustration ☐ Loneliness ☐ Grief

☐ Sadness ☐ Surprise ☐ Jealousy ☐ Disgust ☐ Joy ☐ Happiness

☐ Curiosity ☐ Love ☐ Sexual ☐ _____ ☐ _____   ☐ _____

Key Words/Elements:

Symbols:

People/Spirits:

Place:

Your Role:

Storyline:

☐ Use this journey for future re-entry?

Nugget of Truth:

More Dream Notes:

Title:

Date:

Type: ☐ Lucid ☐ Meditation ☐ Sleeping ☐ Re-Entry
☐ Shamanic Journey ☐ Breathwork

Mood: ☐ Pleasant ☐ Neutral ☐ Unpleasant

Emotions: ☐ Anger ☐ Fear ☐ Frustration ☐ Loneliness ☐ Grief

☐ Sadness ☐ Surprise ☐ Jealousy ☐ Disgust ☐ Joy ☐ Happiness

☐ Curiosity ☐ Love ☐ Sexual ☐ _____ ☐ _____ ☐ _____

Key Words/Elements:

Symbols:

People/Spirits:

Place:

Your Role:

Storyline:

☐ Use this journey for future re-entry?

Nugget of Truth:

More Dream Notes:

Title:

Date:

Type: ☐ Lucid ☐ Meditation ☐ Sleeping ☐ Re-Entry
☐ Shamanic Journey ☐ Breathwork

Mood: ☐ Pleasant ☐ Neutral ☐ Unpleasant

Emotions: ☐ Anger ☐ Fear ☐ Frustration ☐ Loneliness ☐ Grief

☐ Sadness ☐ Surprise ☐ Jealousy ☐ Disgust ☐ Joy ☐ Happiness

☐ Curiosity ☐ Love ☐ Sexual ☐ _____ ☐ _____ ☐ _____

Key Words/Elements:

Symbols:

People/Spirits:

Place:

Your Role:

Storyline:

☐ Use this journey for future re-entry?

Nugget of Truth:

More Dream Notes:

Title:

Date:

Type: ☐ Lucid ☐ Meditation ☐ Sleeping ☐ Re-Entry
☐ Shamanic Journey ☐ Breathwork

Mood: ☐ Pleasant ☐ Neutral ☐ Unpleasant

Emotions: ☐ Anger ☐ Fear ☐ Frustration ☐ Loneliness ☐ Grief

☐ Sadness ☐ Surprise ☐ Jealousy ☐ Disgust ☐ Joy ☐ Happiness

☐ Curiosity ☐ Love ☐ Sexual ☐ _____ ☐ _____ ☐ _____

Key Words/Elements:

Symbols:

People/Spirits:

Place:

Your Role:

Storyline:

☐ Use this journey for future re-entry?

Nugget of Truth:

More Dream Notes:

Title:

Date:

Type: ☐ Lucid   ☐ Meditation ☐ Sleeping ☐ Re-Entry
☐ Shamanic Journey   ☐ Breathwork

Mood: ☐ Pleasant ☐ Neutral ☐ Unpleasant

Emotions: ☐ Anger ☐ Fear ☐ Frustration ☐ Loneliness ☐ Grief

☐ Sadness ☐ Surprise ☐ Jealousy ☐ Disgust ☐ Joy ☐ Happiness

☐ Curiosity ☐ Love ☐ Sexual ☐ _____ ☐ _____ ☐ _____

Key Words/Elements:

Symbols:

People/Spirits:

Place:

Your Role:

Storyline:

☐ Use this journey for future re-entry?

Nugget of Truth:

More Dream Notes:

Title:

Date:

Type: ☐ Lucid   ☐ Meditation ☐ Sleeping ☐ Re-Entry
☐ Shamanic Journey   ☐ Breathwork

Mood: ☐ Pleasant ☐ Neutral ☐ Unpleasant

Emotions: ☐ Anger ☐ Fear ☐ Frustration ☐ Loneliness ☐ Grief

☐ Sadness ☐ Surprise ☐ Jealousy ☐ Disgust ☐ Joy ☐ Happiness

☐ Curiosity ☐ Love ☐ Sexual ☐ _____ ☐ _____ ☐ _____

Key Words/Elements:

Symbols:

People/Spirits:

Place:

Your Role:

Storyline:

☐ Use this journey for future re-entry?

Nugget of Truth:

More Dream Notes:

Title:

Date:

Type: ☐ Lucid ☐ Meditation ☐ Sleeping ☐ Re-Entry
☐ Shamanic Journey ☐ Breathwork

Mood: ☐ Pleasant ☐ Neutral ☐ Unpleasant

Emotions: ☐ Anger ☐ Fear ☐ Frustration ☐ Loneliness ☐ Grief

☐ Sadness ☐ Surprise ☐ Jealousy ☐ Disgust ☐ Joy ☐ Happiness

☐ Curiosity ☐ Love ☐ Sexual ☐ _____ ☐ _____ ☐ _____

Key Words/Elements:

Symbols:

People/Spirits:

Place:

Your Role:

Storyline:

☐ Use this journey for future re-entry?

Nugget of Truth:

More Dream Notes:

Title:

Date:

Type: ☐ Lucid ☐ Meditation ☐ Sleeping ☐ Re-Entry
☐ Shamanic Journey ☐ Breathwork

Mood: ☐ Pleasant ☐ Neutral ☐ Unpleasant

Emotions: ☐ Anger ☐ Fear ☐ Frustration ☐ Loneliness ☐ Grief

☐ Sadness ☐ Surprise ☐ Jealousy ☐ Disgust ☐ Joy ☐ Happiness

☐ Curiosity ☐ Love ☐ Sexual ☐ _____ ☐ _____ ☐ _____

Key Words/Elements:

Symbols:

People/Spirits:

Place:

Your Role:

Storyline:

☐ Use this journey for future re-entry?

Nugget of Truth:

More Dream Notes:

Title:

Date:

Type: ☐ Lucid ☐ Meditation ☐ Sleeping ☐ Re-Entry
☐ Shamanic Journey ☐ Breathwork

Mood: ☐ Pleasant ☐ Neutral ☐ Unpleasant

Emotions: ☐ Anger ☐ Fear ☐ Frustration ☐ Loneliness ☐ Grief

☐ Sadness ☐ Surprise ☐ Jealousy ☐ Disgust ☐ Joy ☐ Happiness

☐ Curiosity ☐ Love ☐ Sexual ☐ _____ ☐ _____ ☐ _____

Key Words/Elements:

Symbols:

People/Spirits:

Place:

Your Role:

Storyline:

☐ Use this journey for future re-entry?

Nugget of Truth:

More Dream Notes:

Title:

Date:

Type: ☐ Lucid   ☐ Meditation   ☐ Sleeping   ☐ Re-Entry
☐ Shamanic Journey   ☐ Breathwork

Mood: ☐ Pleasant   ☐ Neutral   ☐ Unpleasant

Emotions: ☐ Anger ☐ Fear ☐ Frustration ☐ Loneliness ☐ Grief

☐ Sadness ☐ Surprise ☐ Jealousy ☐ Disgust ☐ Joy ☐ Happiness

☐ Curiosity ☐ Love ☐ Sexual ☐ _____ ☐ _____   ☐ _____

Key Words/Elements:

Symbols:

People/Spirits:

Place:

Your Role:

Storyline:

☐ Use this journey for future re-entry?

Nugget of Truth:

More Dream Notes:

Title:

Date:

Type: ☐ Lucid ☐ Meditation ☐ Sleeping ☐ Re-Entry
☐ Shamanic Journey ☐ Breathwork

Mood: ☐ Pleasant ☐ Neutral ☐ Unpleasant

Emotions: ☐ Anger ☐ Fear ☐ Frustration ☐ Loneliness ☐ Grief
☐ Sadness ☐ Surprise ☐ Jealousy ☐ Disgust ☐ Joy ☐ Happiness
☐ Curiosity ☐ Love ☐ Sexual ☐ _____ ☐ _____ ☐ _____

Key Words/Elements:

Symbols:

People/Spirits:

Place:

Your Role:

Storyline:

☐ Use this journey for future re-entry?

Nugget of Truth:

More Dream Notes:

Title:

Date:

Type: ☐ Lucid   ☐ Meditation   ☐ Sleeping   ☐ Re-Entry
☐ Shamanic Journey   ☐ Breathwork

Mood: ☐ Pleasant   ☐ Neutral ☐ Unpleasant

Emotions: ☐ Anger ☐ Fear ☐ Frustration ☐ Loneliness ☐ Grief
☐ Sadness ☐ Surprise ☐ Jealousy ☐ Disgust ☐ Joy ☐ Happiness
☐ Curiosity ☐ Love ☐ Sexual ☐ _____ ☐ _____ ☐ _____

Key Words/Elements:

Symbols:

People/Spirits:

Place:

Your Role:

Storyline:

☐ Use this journey for future re-entry?

Nugget of Truth:

More Dream Notes:

Title:

Date:

Type: ☐ Lucid ☐ Meditation ☐ Sleeping ☐ Re-Entry
☐ Shamanic Journey ☐ Breathwork

Mood: ☐ Pleasant ☐ Neutral ☐ Unpleasant

Emotions: ☐ Anger ☐ Fear ☐ Frustration ☐ Loneliness ☐ Grief

☐ Sadness ☐ Surprise ☐ Jealousy ☐ Disgust ☐ Joy ☐ Happiness

☐ Curiosity ☐ Love ☐ Sexual ☐ _____ ☐ _____ ☐ _____

Key Words/Elements:

Symbols:

People/Spirits:

Place:

Your Role:

Storyline:

☐ Use this journey for future re-entry?

Nugget of Truth:

More Dream Notes:

Title:

Date:

Type: ☐ Lucid ☐ Meditation ☐ Sleeping ☐ Re-Entry
☐ Shamanic Journey ☐ Breathwork

Mood: ☐ Pleasant ☐ Neutral ☐ Unpleasant

Emotions: ☐ Anger ☐ Fear ☐ Frustration ☐ Loneliness ☐ Grief

☐ Sadness ☐ Surprise ☐ Jealousy ☐ Disgust ☐ Joy ☐ Happiness

☐ Curiosity ☐ Love ☐ Sexual ☐ _____ ☐ _____ ☐ _____

Key Words/Elements:

Symbols:

People/Spirits:

Place:

Your Role:

Storyline:

☐ Use this journey for future re-entry?

Nugget of Truth:

More Dream Notes:

Title:

Date:

Type: ☐ Lucid   ☐ Meditation   ☐ Sleeping   ☐ Re-Entry
☐ Shamanic Journey   ☐ Breathwork

Mood: ☐ Pleasant   ☐ Neutral   ☐ Unpleasant

Emotions: ☐ Anger   ☐ Fear ☐ Frustration ☐ Loneliness ☐ Grief

☐ Sadness   ☐ Surprise ☐ Jealousy ☐ Disgust ☐ Joy ☐ Happiness

☐ Curiosity ☐ Love   ☐ Sexual ☐ _____   ☐ _____   ☐ _____

Key Words/Elements:

Symbols:

People/Spirits:

Place:

Your Role:

Storyline:

☐ Use this journey for future re-entry?

Nugget of Truth:

More Dream Notes:

Title:

Date:

Type: ☐ Lucid ☐ Meditation ☐ Sleeping ☐ Re-Entry
☐ Shamanic Journey ☐ Breathwork

Mood: ☐ Pleasant ☐ Neutral ☐ Unpleasant

Emotions: ☐ Anger ☐ Fear ☐ Frustration ☐ Loneliness ☐ Grief

☐ Sadness ☐ Surprise ☐ Jealousy ☐ Disgust ☐ Joy ☐ Happiness

☐ Curiosity ☐ Love ☐ Sexual ☐ _____ ☐ _____ ☐ _____

Key Words/Elements:

Symbols:

People/Spirits:

Place:

Your Role:

Storyline:

☐ Use this journey for future re-entry?

Nugget of Truth:

More Dream Notes:

Title:

Date:

Type: ☐ Lucid   ☐ Meditation   ☐ Sleeping   ☐ Re-Entry
☐ Shamanic Journey   ☐ Breathwork

Mood: ☐ Pleasant   ☐ Neutral   ☐ Unpleasant

Emotions: ☐ Anger ☐ Fear ☐ Frustration ☐ Loneliness ☐ Grief

☐ Sadness   ☐ Surprise ☐ Jealousy ☐ Disgust ☐ Joy ☐ Happiness

☐ Curiosity ☐ Love ☐ Sexual ☐ _____ ☐ _____   ☐ _____

Key Words/Elements:

Symbols:

People/Spirits:

Place:

Your Role:

Storyline:

☐ Use this journey for future re-entry?

Nugget of Truth:

More Dream Notes:

Title:

Date:

Type: ☐ Lucid ☐ Meditation ☐ Sleeping ☐ Re-Entry
☐ Shamanic Journey ☐ Breathwork

Mood: ☐ Pleasant ☐ Neutral ☐ Unpleasant

Emotions: ☐ Anger ☐ Fear ☐ Frustration ☐ Loneliness ☐ Grief

☐ Sadness ☐ Surprise ☐ Jealousy ☐ Disgust ☐ Joy ☐ Happiness

☐ Curiosity ☐ Love ☐ Sexual ☐ _____ ☐ _____ ☐ _____

Key Words/Elements:

Symbols:

People/Spirits:

Place:

Your Role:

Storyline:

☐ Use this journey for future re-entry?

Nugget of Truth:

More Dream Notes:

Title:

Date:

Type: ☐ Lucid ☐ Meditation ☐ Sleeping ☐ Re-Entry
☐ Shamanic Journey ☐ Breathwork

Mood: ☐ Pleasant ☐ Neutral ☐ Unpleasant

Emotions: ☐ Anger ☐ Fear ☐ Frustration ☐ Loneliness ☐ Grief

☐ Sadness ☐ Surprise ☐ Jealousy ☐ Disgust ☐ Joy ☐ Happiness

☐ Curiosity ☐ Love ☐ Sexual ☐ _____ ☐ _____ ☐ _____

Key Words/Elements:

Symbols:

People/Spirits:

Place:

Your Role:

Storyline:

☐ Use this journey for future re-entry?

Nugget of Truth:

More Dream Notes:

Title:

Date:

Type: ☐ Lucid   ☐ Meditation   ☐ Sleeping   ☐ Re-Entry
☐ Shamanic Journey   ☐ Breathwork

Mood: ☐ Pleasant   ☐ Neutral   ☐ Unpleasant

Emotions: ☐ Anger   ☐ Fear   ☐ Frustration   ☐ Loneliness   ☐ Grief

☐ Sadness   ☐ Surprise   ☐ Jealousy   ☐ Disgust   ☐ Joy   ☐ Happiness

☐ Curiosity   ☐ Love   ☐ Sexual   ☐ _____   ☐ _____   ☐ _____

Key Words/Elements:

Symbols:

People/Spirits:

Place:

Your Role:

Storyline:

☐ Use this journey for future re-entry?

Nugget of Truth:

More Dream Notes:

Title:

Date:

Type: ☐ Lucid   ☐ Meditation ☐ Sleeping ☐ Re-Entry
☐ Shamanic Journey   ☐ Breathwork

Mood: ☐ Pleasant ☐ Neutral ☐ Unpleasant

Emotions: ☐ Anger ☐ Fear ☐ Frustration ☐ Loneliness ☐ Grief

☐ Sadness ☐ Surprise ☐ Jealousy ☐ Disgust ☐ Joy ☐ Happiness

☐ Curiosity ☐ Love ☐ Sexual ☐ _____ ☐ _____   ☐ _____

Key Words/Elements:

Symbols:

People/Spirits:

Place:

Your Role:

Storyline:

☐ Use this journey for future re-entry?

Nugget of Truth:

More Dream Notes:

Title:

Date:

Type: ☐ Lucid ☐ Meditation ☐ Sleeping ☐ Re-Entry
☐ Shamanic Journey ☐ Breathwork

Mood: ☐ Pleasant ☐ Neutral ☐ Unpleasant

Emotions: ☐ Anger ☐ Fear ☐ Frustration ☐ Loneliness ☐ Grief

☐ Sadness ☐ Surprise ☐ Jealousy ☐ Disgust ☐ Joy ☐ Happiness

☐ Curiosity ☐ Love ☐ Sexual ☐ _____ ☐ _____ ☐ _____

Key Words/Elements:

Symbols:

People/Spirits:

Place:

Your Role:

Storyline:

☐ Use this journey for future re-entry?

Nugget of Truth:

More Dream Notes:

Title:

Date:

Type: ☐ Lucid   ☐ Meditation   ☐ Sleeping   ☐ Re-Entry
☐ Shamanic Journey   ☐ Breathwork

Mood: ☐ Pleasant   ☐ Neutral   ☐ Unpleasant

Emotions: ☐ Anger ☐ Fear ☐ Frustration ☐ Loneliness ☐ Grief

☐ Sadness ☐ Surprise ☐ Jealousy ☐ Disgust ☐ Joy ☐ Happiness

☐ Curiosity ☐ Love ☐ Sexual ☐ _____ ☐ _____   ☐ _____

Key Words/Elements:

Symbols:

People/Spirits:

Place:

Your Role:

Storyline:

☐ Use this journey for future re-entry?

Nugget of Truth:

More Dream Notes:

Title:

Date:

Type: ☐ Lucid   ☐ Meditation   ☐ Sleeping   ☐ Re-Entry
☐ Shamanic Journey   ☐ Breathwork

Mood: ☐ Pleasant   ☐ Neutral   ☐ Unpleasant

Emotions: ☐ Anger   ☐ Fear ☐ Frustration ☐ Loneliness ☐ Grief

☐ Sadness ☐ Surprise ☐ Jealousy ☐ Disgust ☐ Joy ☐ Happiness

☐ Curiosity ☐ Love ☐ Sexual ☐ _____ ☐ _____ ☐ _____

Key Words/Elements:

Symbols:

People/Spirits:

Place:

Your Role:

Storyline:

☐ Use this journey for future re-entry?

Nugget of Truth:

More Dream Notes:

Title:

Date:

Type: ☐ Lucid ☐ Meditation ☐ Sleeping ☐ Re-Entry
☐ Shamanic Journey ☐ Breathwork

Mood: ☐ Pleasant ☐ Neutral ☐ Unpleasant

Emotions: ☐ Anger ☐ Fear ☐ Frustration ☐ Loneliness ☐ Grief

☐ Sadness ☐ Surprise ☐ Jealousy ☐ Disgust ☐ Joy ☐ Happiness

☐ Curiosity ☐ Love ☐ Sexual ☐ _____ ☐ _____ ☐ _____

Key Words/Elements:

Symbols:

People/Spirits:

Place:

Your Role:

Storyline:

☐ Use this journey for future re-entry?

Nugget of Truth:

More Dream Notes:

Title:

Date:

Type: ☐ Lucid   ☐ Meditation ☐ Sleeping ☐ Re-Entry
☐ Shamanic Journey   ☐ Breathwork

Mood: ☐ Pleasant ☐ Neutral ☐ Unpleasant

Emotions: ☐ Anger ☐ Fear ☐ Frustration ☐ Loneliness ☐ Grief

☐ Sadness ☐ Surprise ☐ Jealousy ☐ Disgust ☐ Joy ☐ Happiness

☐ Curiosity ☐ Love ☐ Sexual ☐ _____ ☐ _____ ☐ _____

Key Words/Elements:

Symbols:

People/Spirits:

Place:

Your Role:

Storyline:

☐ Use this journey for future re-entry?

Nugget of Truth:

More Dream Notes:

Title:

Date:

Type: ☐ Lucid   ☐ Meditation   ☐ Sleeping   ☐ Re-Entry
☐ Shamanic Journey   ☐ Breathwork

Mood: ☐ Pleasant   ☐ Neutral   ☐ Unpleasant

Emotions: ☐ Anger ☐ Fear ☐ Frustration ☐ Loneliness ☐ Grief

☐ Sadness ☐ Surprise ☐ Jealousy ☐ Disgust ☐ Joy ☐ Happiness

☐ Curiosity ☐ Love ☐ Sexual ☐ _____ ☐ _____ ☐ _____

Key Words/Elements:

Symbols:

People/Spirits:

Place:

Your Role:

Storyline:

☐ Use this journey for future re-entry?

Nugget of Truth:

More Dream Notes:

Title:

Date:

Type: ☐ Lucid ☐ Meditation ☐ Sleeping ☐ Re-Entry
☐ Shamanic Journey ☐ Breathwork

Mood: ☐ Pleasant ☐ Neutral ☐ Unpleasant

Emotions: ☐ Anger ☐ Fear ☐ Frustration ☐ Loneliness ☐ Grief

☐ Sadness ☐ Surprise ☐ Jealousy ☐ Disgust ☐ Joy ☐ Happiness

☐ Curiosity ☐ Love ☐ Sexual ☐ _____ ☐ _____ ☐ _____

Key Words/Elements:

Symbols:

People/Spirits:

Place:

Your Role:

Storyline:

☐ Use this journey for future re-entry?

Nugget of Truth:

More Dream Notes:

Title:

Date:

Type: ☐ Lucid ☐ Meditation ☐ Sleeping ☐ Re-Entry
☐ Shamanic Journey ☐ Breathwork

Mood: ☐ Pleasant ☐ Neutral ☐ Unpleasant

Emotions: ☐ Anger ☐ Fear ☐ Frustration ☐ Loneliness ☐ Grief

☐ Sadness ☐ Surprise ☐ Jealousy ☐ Disgust ☐ Joy ☐ Happiness

☐ Curiosity ☐ Love ☐ Sexual ☐ _____ ☐ _____ ☐ _____

Key Words/Elements:

Symbols:

People/Spirits:

Place:

Your Role:

Storyline:

☐ Use this journey for future re-entry?

Nugget of Truth:

More Dream Notes:

Title:

Date:

Type: ☐ Lucid ☐ Meditation ☐ Sleeping ☐ Re-Entry
☐ Shamanic Journey ☐ Breathwork

Mood: ☐ Pleasant ☐ Neutral ☐ Unpleasant

Emotions: ☐ Anger ☐ Fear ☐ Frustration ☐ Loneliness ☐ Grief

☐ Sadness ☐ Surprise ☐ Jealousy ☐ Disgust ☐ Joy ☐ Happiness

☐ Curiosity ☐ Love ☐ Sexual ☐ _____ ☐ _____ ☐ _____

Key Words/Elements:

Symbols:

People/Spirits:

Place:

Your Role:

Storyline:

☐ Use this journey for future re-entry?

Nugget of Truth:

More Dream Notes:

Title:

Date:

Type: ☐ Lucid ☐ Meditation ☐ Sleeping ☐ Re-Entry
☐ Shamanic Journey ☐ Breathwork

Mood: ☐ Pleasant ☐ Neutral ☐ Unpleasant

Emotions: ☐ Anger ☐ Fear ☐ Frustration ☐ Loneliness ☐ Grief

☐ Sadness ☐ Surprise ☐ Jealousy ☐ Disgust ☐ Joy ☐ Happiness

☐ Curiosity ☐ Love ☐ Sexual ☐ _____ ☐ _____ ☐ _____

Key Words/Elements:

Symbols:

People/Spirits:

Place:

Your Role:

Storyline:

☐ Use this journey for future re-entry?

Nugget of Truth:

More Dream Notes:

Title:

Date:

Type: ☐ Lucid ☐ Meditation ☐ Sleeping ☐ Re-Entry
☐ Shamanic Journey ☐ Breathwork

Mood: ☐ Pleasant ☐ Neutral ☐ Unpleasant

Emotions: ☐ Anger ☐ Fear ☐ Frustration ☐ Loneliness ☐ Grief

☐ Sadness ☐ Surprise ☐ Jealousy ☐ Disgust ☐ Joy ☐ Happiness

☐ Curiosity ☐ Love ☐ Sexual ☐ _____ ☐ _____ ☐ _____

Key Words/Elements:

Symbols:

People/Spirits:

Place:

Your Role:

Storyline:

☐ Use this journey for future re-entry?

Nugget of Truth:

More Dream Notes:

Title:

Date:

Type: ☐ Lucid   ☐ Meditation   ☐ Sleeping   ☐ Re-Entry
☐ Shamanic Journey   ☐ Breathwork

Mood: ☐ Pleasant   ☐ Neutral ☐ Unpleasant

Emotions: ☐ Anger ☐ Fear ☐ Frustration ☐ Loneliness ☐ Grief

☐ Sadness ☐ Surprise ☐ Jealousy ☐ Disgust ☐ Joy ☐ Happiness

☐ Curiosity ☐ Love ☐ Sexual ☐ _____ ☐ _____   ☐ _____

Key Words/Elements:

Symbols:

People/Spirits:

Place:

Your Role:

Storyline:

☐ Use this journey for future re-entry?

Nugget of Truth:

More Dream Notes:

Title:

Date:

Type: ☐ Lucid   ☐ Meditation   ☐ Sleeping   ☐ Re-Entry
☐ Shamanic Journey   ☐ Breathwork

Mood: ☐ Pleasant   ☐ Neutral   ☐ Unpleasant

Emotions: ☐ Anger   ☐ Fear   ☐ Frustration   ☐ Loneliness   ☐ Grief

☐ Sadness   ☐ Surprise ☐ Jealousy ☐ Disgust ☐ Joy ☐ Happiness

☐ Curiosity ☐ Love   ☐ Sexual ☐ _____   ☐ _____   ☐ _____

Key Words/Elements:

Symbols:

People/Spirits:

Place:

Your Role:

Storyline:

☐ Use this journey for future re-entry?

Nugget of Truth:

More Dream Notes:

Title:

Date:

Type: ☐ Lucid ☐ Meditation ☐ Sleeping ☐ Re-Entry
☐ Shamanic Journey ☐ Breathwork

Mood: ☐ Pleasant ☐ Neutral ☐ Unpleasant

Emotions: ☐ Anger ☐ Fear ☐ Frustration ☐ Loneliness ☐ Grief

☐ Sadness ☐ Surprise ☐ Jealousy ☐ Disgust ☐ Joy ☐ Happiness

☐ Curiosity ☐ Love ☐ Sexual ☐ _____ ☐ _____ ☐ _____

Key Words/Elements:

Symbols:

People/Spirits:

Place:

Your Role:

Storyline:

☐ Use this journey for future re-entry?

Nugget of Truth:

More Dream Notes:

Title:

Date:

Type: ☐ Lucid ☐ Meditation ☐ Sleeping ☐ Re-Entry
☐ Shamanic Journey ☐ Breathwork

Mood: ☐ Pleasant ☐ Neutral ☐ Unpleasant

Emotions: ☐ Anger ☐ Fear ☐ Frustration ☐ Loneliness ☐ Grief

☐ Sadness ☐ Surprise ☐ Jealousy ☐ Disgust ☐ Joy ☐ Happiness

☐ Curiosity ☐ Love ☐ Sexual ☐ _____ ☐ _____ ☐ _____

Key Words/Elements:

Symbols:

People/Spirits:

Place:

Your Role:

Storyline:

☐ Use this journey for future re-entry?

Nugget of Truth:

More Dream Notes:

Title:

Date:

Type: ☐ Lucid ☐ Meditation ☐ Sleeping ☐ Re-Entry
☐ Shamanic Journey ☐ Breathwork

Mood: ☐ Pleasant ☐ Neutral ☐ Unpleasant

Emotions: ☐ Anger ☐ Fear ☐ Frustration ☐ Loneliness ☐ Grief

☐ Sadness ☐ Surprise ☐ Jealousy ☐ Disgust ☐ Joy ☐ Happiness

☐ Curiosity ☐ Love ☐ Sexual ☐ _____ ☐ _____ ☐ _____

Key Words/Elements:

Symbols:

People/Spirits:

Place:

Your Role:

Storyline:

☐ Use this journey for future re-entry?

Nugget of Truth:

More Dream Notes:

Title:

Date:

Type: ☐ Lucid ☐ Meditation ☐ Sleeping ☐ Re-Entry
☐ Shamanic Journey ☐ Breathwork

Mood: ☐ Pleasant ☐ Neutral ☐ Unpleasant

Emotions: ☐ Anger ☐ Fear ☐ Frustration ☐ Loneliness ☐ Grief

☐ Sadness ☐ Surprise ☐ Jealousy ☐ Disgust ☐ Joy ☐ Happiness

☐ Curiosity ☐ Love ☐ Sexual ☐ _____ ☐ _____ ☐ _____

Key Words/Elements:

Symbols:

People/Spirits:

Place:

Your Role:

Storyline:

☐ Use this journey for future re-entry?

Messages from Our Spirit Guides

In dreams and journeys our Helping Spirits and Guides give us many messages. Sometimes those messages are repeated time and time again but in our 3rd dimensional "self" we forget.

The following pages are for you to record specific messages you receive during your journeys and to create profile pages of each of your Spirit Guides. You can continue to add information as you get to know them throughout your journeys. When compiled into one place, you will begin to notice patterns and repeated messages as well as to know your Spirit Guides more deeply.

Working with your Spirit Guides is a deeply beautiful experience. They speak to us many different ways, many languages that only the soul truly understands.

Spirit Guide Profile

Use this space to paste any images, drawings, words, etc. which remind you of this Spirit Guide.

Spirit Guide Profile

Name of Guide: _____

What kind of Guide are they for you?

☐ Primary Guide   ☐ Helping Spirit   ☐ Power Animal   ☐ Ancestor

Describe this Guide

What does their energy feel like?

_____

_____

Do you sense they are male or female?

How many lifetimes has this Guide been with you?

What is their primary message for you?

_____

What are they here to help you with?

_____

What gift do they give you?

_____

What signs do they give you in this reality to show you they are present?

_____

_____

When are you to call on this Guide?

_____

_____

Spirit Guide Profile

Use this space to paste any images, drawings, words, etc. which remind you of this Spirit Guide.

Spirit Guide Profile

Name of Guide: _____

What kind of Guide are they for you?

☐ Primary Guide   ☐ Helping Spirit   ☐ Power Animal   ☐ Ancestor

Describe this Guide

What does their energy feel like?

_____

_____

Do you sense they are male or female?

How many lifetimes has this Guide been with you?

What is their primary message for you?

_____

What are they here to help you with?

_____

What gift do they give you?

_____

What signs do they give you in this reality to show you they are present?

_____

_____

When are you to call on this Guide?

_____

_____

Spirit Guide Profile

Use this space to paste any images, drawings, words, etc. which remind you of this Spirit Guide.

Spirit Guide Profile

Name of Guide: _____

What kind of Guide are they for you?

☐ Primary Guide ☐ Helping Spirit ☐ Power Animal ☐ Ancestor

Describe this Guide

What does their energy feel like?

_____

_____

Do you sense they are male or female?

How many lifetimes has this Guide been with you?

What is their primary message for you?

_____

What are they here to help you with?

_____

What gift do they give you?

_____

What signs do they give you in this reality to show you they are present?

_____

_____

When are you to call on this Guide?

_____

_____

Spirit Guide Profile

Use this space to paste any images, drawings, words, etc. which remind you of this Spirit Guide.

Spirit Guide Profile

Name of Guide: _____

What kind of Guide are they for you?

☐ Primary Guide ☐ Helping Spirit ☐ Power Animal ☐ Ancestor

Describe this Guide

What does their energy feel like?

Do you sense they are male or female?

How many lifetimes has this Guide been with you?

What is their primary message for you?

What are they here to help you with?

What gift do they give you?

What signs do they give you in this reality to show you they are present?

When are you to call on this Guide?

Spirit Guide Profile

Use this space to paste any images, drawings, words, etc. which remind you of this Spirit Guide.

Spirit Guide Profile

Name of Guide: _____

What kind of Guide are they for you?

☐ Primary Guide ☐ Helping Spirit ☐ Power Animal ☐ Ancestor

Describe this Guide

What does their energy feel like?

Do you sense they are male or female?

How many lifetimes has this Guide been with you?

What is their primary message for you?

What are they here to help you with?

What gift do they give you?

What signs do they give you in this reality to show you they are present?

When are you to call on this Guide?

Date	Guide	Message

Messages From Your Helping Spirits

Date	Guide	Message

Date	Guide	Message

Date	Guide	Message

Date	Guide	Message

Date	Guide	Message

About Dakota Earth Cloud Walker

Dakota Earth Cloud Walker has been in the field of holistic Medicine and Shamanic work for over 20 years. Dakota is a Certified Shamanic Breathwork Practitioner, Shamanic Coach, Trance Dance Facilitator, and a Quantum Shamanic Practitioner.

She, along with her partner Amber, own Sacred Soul Center and Gaia Wisdom Sanctuary located in the heart of the Appalachian Mountains near Todd, North Carolina . Their work extends not only to their local community but to a global community as well.

More information on the Shamanic Coaching and Master Shamanic Practitioner Program along with the Shamanic Journeyer's Club can be found online at:
www.sacredsoulcenter.com

Made in the USA
Middletown, DE
29 September 2017